NO-COOK COOKERY

NO-COOK COOKERY

Delicious dishes that need no cooking

SACKVILLE BOOKS

First published in 1987
by Sackville Books Ltd
Sackville House
78 Margaret Street, London W1N 7HB

© Sackville Design Group Ltd 1987

Designed and produced by Sackville Design Group Ltd
Typeset in Bembo by Optima Typographic Limited

Art director: Al Rockall
Editor: Heather Thomas
Photographs: David Burch

British Library Cataloguing in Publication Data
Faldo, Melanie
No-cook cookery.
1. Cookery
I. Title II. Rhodes, Lorna
641.5'55   TX652

ISBN 0-94861-510-9

Printed and bound in Spain by Graficromo, S.A., Cordoba

Recipes
*Note that all the recipes throughout are to serve 4
people only unless otherwise specified.*

Contents

Introduction

For many years, most people's idea of no-cook cooking was to delve into their kitchen cupboards and open cans and packets, thus making use of processed and ready prepared foods. However, we have come a long way since the days of high-tech convenience; it is almost as if people want to get back to the origins of preparing food. Being realistic, there are not many of us who have the time to spend in the kitchen these days, and yet we still want to prepare delicious meals for our family and friends. Today there is more emphasis on healthy eating because public awareness of potentially harmful chemical additives in processed foods has encouraged us to use fresher, more nutritious ingredients, often in their raw, uncooked state. That is not to say that we should never open a can as there are some marvellous store cupboard standbys.

There is probably no such thing as a truly original recipe and the underlying theme of this book is to show interesting new combinations of ingredients – it is unique in so far as none of the dishes require any cooking. In fact, the nearest you get to cooking is to boil some water for blanching vegetables, melting chocolate or dissolving gelatine. Whether you are accustomed to taking advantage of speciality foods from delicatessen counters or have less extravagant tastes, here is an opportunity to explore the unusual and exotic fruits and vegetables which are now available in many supermarkets.

The magic and essential ingredient of uncooked food is freshness. Thus it is essential to choose really fresh fish, salad vegetables or fruits; and if the quality of the ingredients is top grade you cannot fail to produce a delicious dish. Raw food is usually more nutritious than cooked food as it retains many important nutrients which can be destroyed by heat.

All the recipes are easy to prepare and require no special skills. You need not be afraid of trying out a new dish, however sensational it may look. And your family and friends will be suitably impressed by the stunning results. This new way of preparing and serving food is even less time-consuming and more convenient if you take legitimate shortcuts and make maximum use of gadgets and kitchen appliances. A good blender or food processor can save you time and labour.

If you are particularly busy, have a demanding job and little time to cook, you will quickly discover that '**No-cook Cookery**' is the naturally easy way to prepare food. For everyone who appreciates good food, it proves the point that healthy eating can be attractive without sacrificing flavour and texture. The recipes reflect the best of current cooking trends, especially in *nouvelle cuisine* and *cuisine naturelle*. In fact, this is the perfect cookery book for all busy men and women who enjoy delicious, healthy food and entertaining but have little time to indulge in preparing cooked feasts.

Appetizers

Crisp and crunchy, colourful crudités offset the smooth creaminess of the aiolli, anchovy and herbed cheese dips.

A trio of dips

Aiolli
3 cloves garlic, crushed
1 egg + 1 egg yolk
pinch of salt
300ml / 10 floz olive oil
2.5ml / ½ teaspoon lemon juice

Mash the crushed garlic, add the egg and salt, then gradually add the oil in a thin trickle, whisking all the time. Add more oil in a steady stream and finally the lemon juice.

Italian anchovy dip
45g / 1¾oz can anchovy fillets, drained
1 clove garlic
30ml / 2 tablespoons olive oil
15ml / 1 tablespoon tomato purée
45ml / 3 tablespoons mayonnaise

Put all the ingredients into a blender or food processor and work until smooth.

Herbed cheese dip
175g / 6oz low-fat soft cheese
30ml / 2 tablespoons natural yoghurt
15ml / 1 tablespoon each snipped chives, parsley,
dill and chervil
pinch of cayenne pepper

Put all the ingredients into a bowl and mix thoroughly before serving with the crudités.

Orange juice and tomatoes make unusual but delicious bedfellows in this refreshing chilled summer soup.

Summer tomato and orange soup

1kg / 2lb ripe tomatoes
15ml / 1 tablespoon sugar
2.5ml / ½ teaspoon salt
5ml / 1 teaspoon onion juice
grated rind and juice of 1 orange
300ml / ½ pint cold whipping cream
Garnish
chopped or sprig basil
30ml / 2 tablespoons whipping cream

Roughly chop the tomatoes and put them in a blender or processor. Work to make a purée. Press the purée through a sieve, discarding the skin and seeds. Add the rest of the ingredients and whisk together until smooth. Allow to chill before serving. Garnish with chopped basil or a single sprig and a good swirl of cream.
Note: to make onion juice, grate a little onion into a filter paper and then squeeze gently to extract the juice.

*Elegant cucumber soup is subtly
flavoured with a hint of fresh mint and
is then chilled to perfection.*

Chilled cucumber soup

1 large cucumber, peeled and finely chopped
sea salt
900ml / 1½ pints thick yoghurt,
preferably goat's milk
1-2 cloves garlic, crushed
30ml / 2 tablespoons chopped fresh mint
salt and white pepper

Put the diced cucumber in a colander, sprinkle with the sea salt and leave to stand for 1 hour. Press the cucumber with your hands to extract as much liquid as possible. Meanwhile, put the yoghurt in a bowl and whisk in the garlic and half of the mint. Stir in the cucumber, season to taste, then refrigerate for at least 2 hours before serving. Garnish the chilled soup with the rest of the mint.

Gazpacho

550g / 1.2lb jar Passata (sieved tomatoes)
2 cloves garlic
½ cucumber, peeled and chopped
1 green pepper, seeded and chopped
1 red pepper, seeded and chopped
50g / 2oz breadcrumbs
15ml / 1 tablespoon chopped parsley
30ml / 2 tablespoons olive oil
30ml / 2 tablespoons red wine vinegar
salt and freshly ground black pepper
1.25ml / ¼ teaspoon dried marjoram
Garnish
ice cubes
1 onion, finely chopped
2 hard-boiled eggs, chopped
12 olives, green or black, stoned and chopped

Put all the ingredients into a blender or food processor, in two batches if necessary, and blend until smooth. Season with salt and pepper. The soup should be the consistency of single cream – if it is too thick, add a little iced water. Turn the soup into a tureen and chill in the refrigerator for at least 1 hour.

Just before serving, add a few ice cubes. Serve accompanied by the different garnishes in small dishes.

Mexican avocado soup

2 large ripe avocados
juice of 1 lime
1 clove garlic, crushed
450ml / 15 floz chicken stock
300ml / 10 floz single cream
salt and freshly ground black pepper
Garnish
thin slices of lime
fresh coriander
tortilla chips (optional)

Peel and stone the avocados and put the flesh and lime juice into a blender or food processor. Blend until smooth. Add the garlic, chicken stock and cream, season with salt and pepper and whisk together once more. Chill for at least 2 hours or overnight to allow the flavours to blend. Serve in soup bowls and garnish each with a slice of lime and a sprig of fresh coriander, accompanied with tortilla chips (optional).

*Glistening beads of red lumpfish add
a colourful Scandinavian
flourish to a light summer salmon pâté.*

Smoked salmon pâté

175g / 6oz smoked salmon trimmings
100g / 4oz curd cheese
juice of ½ lemon
60ml / 4 tablespoons Greek yoghurt
freshly ground black pepper
Garnish
lemon slices
red lumpfish
melba toast

Put the smoked salmon, curd cheese, lemon juice and yoghurt in a blender or food processor and work until smooth. Season to taste, then turn into either 4 individual dishes or one larger serving dish and chill before serving. Serve garnished with lemon slices and a little red lumpfish with melba toast.

*Tender artichoke bottoms are
topped with a swirl of pâté and enhanced
by a fan of emerald mange-tout.*

Stuffed artichokes

400g / 14 oz can artichoke bottoms
175g / 6 oz low-fat chicken liver pâté
15ml / 1 tablespoon brandy
45ml / 3 tablespoons crème fraiche
salt and freshly ground pepper
100g / 4 oz mange-tout
thin strips of red pepper

Drain the artichoke bottoms and place on a piece of kitchen paper. Put the pâté into a blender or food processor with the brandy and crème fraiche. Season and blend together. Place the mixture in a piping bag fitted with a star nozzle and pipe the mixture into the artichoke bottoms.

Trim the mange-tout and put them in a bowl. Pour over boiling water and stand for 2 minutes. Rinse under cold water and drain well. Arrange the mange-tout on plates and sit the stuffed artichokes on top. Decorate the pâté with thin strips of red pepper.

Note: if you cannot obtain artichoke bottoms, you could substitute tomatoes. Just cut off the tops and hollow them out, removing the seeds. Fill with piped pâté in the same way.

*Spicy sardine pâté is served
seductively in a spiky lemon for a really
sophisticated appetizer course.*

Sardine nests

2 large lemons
125g / 4oz sardines in oil, drained
50g / 2oz cream cheese
30ml / 2 tablespoons soured cream
2.5ml / ½ teaspoon curry powder
5ml / 1 teaspoon Worcestershire sauce
freshly ground black pepper
25g / 1oz wholemeal breadcrumbs
10ml / 2 teaspoons lemon juice
parsley and tomato wedges to garnish

Carefully cut the lemons in half in a zigzag fashion and scoop out the pulp with a serrated edge knife, reserving the juice and pulp. Trim the bottoms of the lemon halves to stand them upright.

Mash the sardines to a paste with the cream cheese, soured cream, curry powder, Worcestershire sauce and pepper to taste. Stir in the breadcrumbs and lemon juice, and pile the sardine filling into the lemon shells. Chill until required and serve garnished with parsley and tomato wedges. Serve with melba toast or Scandinavian crispbreads.

Smoked mackerel pâté with horseradish sauce

225g / 8oz smoked mackerel fillets
225g / 8oz curd cheese
juice of ½ lemon
freshly ground black pepper
Horseradish sauce
15ml / 1 tablespoon horseradish sauce
45ml / 3 tablespoons natural yoghurt
5ml / 1 teaspoon chopped dill
Garnish
cucumber slices

Skin the mackerel and remove any bones. Put the fish in a food processor with the curd cheese and lemon juice and blend together. Season with black pepper. Turn the pâté into a small loaf tin lined with greaseproof paper and chill overnight.

Make the sauce by mixing the horseradish sauce with the yoghurt and dill. Carefully turn the pâté out of the tin and remove the paper. Cut off slices and arrange on individual serving plates with a spoonful of sauce. Garnish with slices of cucumber.

Spiced bean dip

425g / 15 oz can red kidney beans
45ml / 3 tablespoons olive oil
2.5ml / ½ teaspoon Tabasco sauce
2.5ml / ½ teaspoon Worcestershire sauce
1 clove garlic, crushed
pinch of ground coriander
tortilla chips

Drain the beans and put all the ingredients into a blender or food processor and blend to a smooth paste. Spoon into an attractive serving bowl and serve with tortilla chips as an appetizer or with drinks before a meal.
Note: you can use dried instead of canned kidney beans. Soak and cook in the usual way before puréeing the beans.

*A*n island of creamy chicken
mousse nestles in a pink sea of tarragon
flavoured tomato coulis.

Cucumber and Stilton mousses

7.5cm / 3 in piece cucumber, thinly sliced
½ cucumber, peeled and finely diced
salt
10ml / 2 teaspoons gelatine
45ml / 3 tablespoons chicken stock
50g / 2oz cream cheese
100g / 4oz blue Stilton, crumbled
30ml / 2 tablespoons mayonnaise
75ml / 5 tablespoons double cream
Garnish
watercress sprigs
shredded lettuce

Halve the thin slices of cucumber and arrange overlapping on the inside of 4 ramekin dishes. Put the diced cucumber in a sieve or colander, sprinkle with salt and set aside for 30 minutes. Dissolve the gelatine in the chicken stock, then set aside to cool. In a bowl, beat the cheeses together until soft and then beat in the mayonnaise. Drain the cucumber and spread over some kitchen paper to absorb any excess moisture. Stir into the cheese mixture with the gelatine. Whip the cream until thick and fold into the mousse. Divide between the 4 ramekins and refrigerate for about 2 hours until set.

To serve the cucumber mousse, turn onto plates and garnish with sprigs of watercress and shredded lettuce.

*Pungent summer herbs in a piquant
tomato sauce complement the smooth creaminess
of pale green avocado mousse.*

Avocado mousse with tomato sauce

12.5g / ½oz gelatine
45ml / 3 tablespoons water
2 large ripe avocados, peeled and stoned
15ml / 1 tablespoon lemon juice
150ml / 5floz cold chicken stock
dash Tabasco sauce
60ml / 4 tablespoons mayonnaise
salt and freshly ground black pepper
150ml / 5floz double cream, whipped
1 egg white, stiffly whipped
flat-leaved parsley to garnish
Sauce
225g / 8oz ripe tomatoes, skinned and seeded
15ml / 1 tablespoon each finely chopped chervil,
parsley and tarragon
2.5ml / ½ teaspoon Worcestershire sauce
10ml / 2 teaspoons lemon juice
15ml / 1 tablespoon mayonnaise
5ml / 1 teaspoon tomato purée

Sprinkle the gelatine over the water; dissolve over a pan of hot water. Mash the avocado with the lemon juice. Beat in the chicken stock, Tabasco and mayonnaise. Season and fold in the gelatine. Fold in the cream and egg white. Pour into a wetted loaf tin and leave in the refrigerator to set.

Work all the sauce ingredients in a blender or food processor. Turn the mousse out and slice. Serve with the sauce and parsley.

Gleaming red pomegranate jewels,
nestling in soured cream and chopped egg
all crown a spicy Mexican guacamole

Guacamole mountains

2 ripe avocados
30ml / 2 tablespoons fresh lime or lemon juice
1 clove garlic, crushed
2 tomatoes, skinned and finely chopped
5 spring onions, chopped
1 green chilli, seeded and finely chopped
15ml / 1 tablespoon chopped fresh coriander leaves
salt and freshly ground black pepper
2 hard-boiled eggs
150ml / 5 fl oz soured cream
pinch of chilli powder
½ pomegranate, seeds removed

Cut the avocados in half, remove the stones and scoop out the flesh into a bowl. Mash with the lime or lemon juice. Add the garlic, chopped tomato, spring onion, chilli and coriander and season with salt and pepper. Divide the guacamole between 4 serving plates and sprinkle with chopped egg. Spoon the soured cream over the top, leaving a border of egg and sprinkle with bright red pomegranate seeds. Serve with corn or tortilla chips.

A sharp dill and mustard sauce accompanies this traditional Scandinavian dish of marinated fresh salmon.

Gravlax

750g / 1½lb tail piece of salmon
30ml / 2 tablespoons coarse sea salt
15ml / 1 tablespoon black peppercorns, crushed
30ml / 2 tablespoons caster sugar
1 large bunch fresh dill, chopped
Sauce
45ml / 3 tablespoons mild mustard
45ml / 3 tablespoons sunflower oil
15ml / 1 tablespoon red wine vinegar
30ml / 2 tablespoons chopped fresh dill
15ml / 1 tablespoon caster sugar
salt and freshly ground black pepper

Bone the salmon, and wipe the fillets with absorbent paper. Mix the salt, peppercorns and sugar and put about one-third in a shallow dish. Lay one salmon fillet skin side down in the dish and sprinkle with the remaining mixture. Cover with dill and lay the other salmon fillet on top. Cover with foil, put a dish on top and weight it down to press the salmon pieces together. Refrigerate for 2-3 days, turning the fish occasionally.

Beat all the sauce ingredients together until the sugar dissolves. To serve the gravlax: scrape the peppercorns and dill off the fish and cut into thin slices as shown opposite. Discard the skin and arrange the slices on individual serving plates. Serve the sauce separately.

Marinated kipper salad

2 kipper fillets, skinned
15ml / 1 tablespoon lemon juice
60ml / 4 tablespoons olive oil
1 red skinned onion, thinly sliced
1 bay leaf
½ crisp lettuce, shredded
1 red dessert apple, cored and diced
2 celery sticks, sliced
5 cm / 2 in piece cucumber, diced

Cut the kipper fillets into thin strips and place in a shallow dish. Mix the lemon juice and oil together and pour over the kipper pieces. Scatter with the onion and bay leaf, then cover and marinate for at least 24 hours or up to a week in the refrigerator.

To serve: arrange the shredded lettuce on a serving dish. Mix the apple, celery and cucumber with the kipper fillets (discarding the bay leaf) and pile on top of the lettuce.

Marinated salmon with ginger

350g / 12oz fresh salmon
120ml / 4floz white wine vinegar
15ml / 1 tablespoon soy sauce
15ml / 1 tablespoon root ginger, cut into slivers
1 clove garlic
Garnish
curly endive
4 thin spring onions
roasted black sesame seeds (or white)

Cut the salmon into thin strips and place in a shallow dish. Pour over the vinegar and soy sauce and then mix in the ginger and garlic. Cover the dish and leave in the refrigerator overnight.

To serve, drain the fish from the marinade and divide between 4 serving plates. Garnish with the endive. Cut each end of the spring onions several times and leave in iced water until they curl attractively. Place a spring onion tassel on each plate and sprinkle with the roasted black sesame seeds.

Succulent crabmeat is tossed with chunks of refreshing cucumber in a spicy ginger and chilli oriental dressing

Chinese crab and cucumber hors d'oeuvre

½ cucumber, peeled
175g / 6oz can crab in brine (white meat), drained
½ red pepper, seeded and finely diced
Dressing
30ml / 2 tablespoons mayonnaise
15ml / 1 tablespoon soy sauce
5ml / 1 teaspoon sesame oil
2.5ml / ½ teaspoon chilli sauce
2.5ml / ½ teaspoon ground ginger
Garnish
175g / 6oz beansprouts, roots trimmed
15ml / 1 tablespoon toasted sesame seeds
snipped chives

Cut the cucumber in quarters lengthways. Remove the seeds and cut the flesh into 5mm / ¼in chunks. Place in a bowl with the crabmeat and red pepper and mix together. Blend the dressing ingredients, pour over the salad and toss well. Refrigerate the salad for 1 hour to allow the flavours to mingle.

To serve, divide the beansprouts between 4 serving plates and spoon the crab salad on top. Sprinkle with the sesame seeds and chives.

Seafood cocktail

1 lettuce, finely shredded
225g / 8oz peeled prawns
Dressing
150ml / 5floz mayonnaise
15ml / 1 tablespoon tomato ketchup
5ml / 1 teaspoon lemon juice
2.5ml / ½ teaspoon French mustard
dash of Worcestershire sauce
dash of Tabasco sauce
salt and freshly ground black pepper
Garnish
paprika pepper
8 unpeeled prawns
4 small lemon wedges

Half fill 4 sundae glasses with shredded lettuce and divide the peeled prawns between them. Mix the dressing ingredients together and spoon over the prawns. Sprinkle the top of each with a little paprika, then decorate the glasses with the unpeeled prawns and wedges of lemon.

Note: for an extra-special cocktail, use lobster or crabmeat.

Egg and prawn soufflés

3 hard-boiled eggs, finely chopped
100g / 4oz peeled prawns, chopped
2 spring onions, finely chopped
30ml / 2 tablespoons mayonnaise
45ml / 3 tablespoons soured cream
10ml / 2 teaspoons gelatine
45ml / 3 tablespoons water
salt and milled pepper
cayenne pepper
1 egg white
Garnish
1 hard-boiled egg, sliced
a few peeled prawns

Put the chopped egg, prawns and spring onions into a bowl and mix well. Blend the mayonnaise and soured cream together. Sprinkle the gelatine onto the water and dissolve in a basin over a pan of hot water. Cool the gelatine slightly and then whisk into the mayonnaise and cream. Stir into the egg mixture. Season with salt, pepper and cayenne, then chill until just beginning to set. Whisk the egg white until stiff and fold it into the soufflé mixture. Turn into 4 individual ramekin dishes and refrigerate until set. Garnish with slices of hard-boiled egg and prawns.

A mixture of succulent oyster and
button mushrooms with green peppercorns
for the most unusual of hors d'oeuvres.

Mushrooms with green peppercorn dressing

175g / 6oz button mushrooms
100g / 4oz oyster mushrooms
2 spring onions, finely chopped
Dressing
90ml / 6 tablespoons olive oil
30ml / 2 tablespoons white wine vinegar
1.25ml / ¼ teaspoon mustard powder
pinch of sugar
5ml / 1 teaspoon green peppercorns in brine,
drained and slightly crushed

Wipe the button mushrooms, trim the stalks and slice. Tear the oyster mushrooms into smaller pieces and place in a bowl with the sliced mushrooms. In a cup, put the oil, vinegar, mustard powder, sugar and peppercorns. Whisk with a fork and pour over the mushrooms. Toss them well, making sure that all the mushrooms are covered with the dressing. Cover the dish and leave to marinate for 1 hour. Sprinkle with the chopped onion and serve.

Note: if you cannot find any oyster mushrooms, substitute peeled prawns. You can also use green peppercorn mustard instead of green peppercorns in the dressing.

*Exotic, scented mango makes
an excellent foil for paper-thin dry cured
Italian beef in a fruity dressing.*

Bresaola and mango appetizer

2 heads chicory
75g / 3oz Bresaola, cut into strips
1 large ripe mango
60ml / 4 tablespoons sunflower oil
15ml / 1 tablespoon white wine vinegar
pinch of mixed spice
pinch of sugar
chopped parsley

Shred the chicory and place in a bowl with the strips of Bresaola. Peel the mango and cut half the flesh into small dice. Place the rest of the fruit in a blender or processor with the oil, vinegar, spice and sugar. Blend the ingredients together to make a smooth dressing. Pour over the salad and toss together. Arrange on 4 plates and garnish with the diced mango and chopped parsley.

Stuffed egg tapenade

100g / 4oz black olives, stoned
50g / 1¾oz can anchovies, rinsed and drained
30ml / 2 tablespoons capers, drained
10ml / 2 teaspoons lemon juice
10ml / 2 teaspoons brandy
2.5ml / ½ teaspoon Dijon mustard
60ml / 4 tablespoons green olive oil
6 hard-boiled eggs, shelled
shredded lettuce
stuffed olives, sliced

Put the olives, anchovies, capers, lemon juice, brandy and mustard in a blender or processor and work to a smooth paste. Gradually add the oil in a steady stream to give a smooth consistency. Spoon into a jar or container, then cover and store in the refrigerator.

Cut the eggs in half and scoop out the yolks into a bowl. Add 30ml/2 tablespoons of the tapenade and mash together to give a smooth filling. Place in a piping bag fitted with a star nozzle and pipe into the egg white, arrange on a bed of shredded lettuce and garnish the eggs with slices of stuffed olives.

Note: you can store the remaining tapenade in the refrigerator for up to three months. Use it as a topping for canapés or a filling for sandwiches.

Mock caviar croustades

15ml / 1 tablespoon chopped dill
150ml / 5 floz soured cream, chilled
salt and freshly ground black pepper
24 small croustade shells
100g / 3½oz jar lumpfish, chilled
sprigs of dill

Mix the chopped dill into the soured cream, season with salt and pepper, and then carefully place a teaspoonful in each croustade shell. Spoon in the lumpfish and garnish with tiny sprigs of dill. Chill until you are ready to serve the croustades, but be sure to eat them within an hour or the shells will become soft.
Note: you can buy croustade cases at most delicatessens and specialist food shops.

A crescent of ruby grapefruit and avocado slices are sprinkled generously with a tangy lime dressing.

Avocado and citrus appetizer

2 avocados
lemon juice
2 pink grapefruit
Dressing
juice and grated rind of 1 lime
2.5ml / ½ teaspoon Dijon mustard
10ml / 2 teaspoons sunflower oil
salt and freshly ground pepper
Garnish
4 thin slices of lime

Cut the avocados in half, twist to separate and remove the stones and peel. Cut each half into 5 slices and brush with lemon juice. Cut away all the skin and pith from the grapefruit and cut into segments. On each plate arrange the slices of avocado and grapefruit alternately (see picture opposite). Mix the dressing ingredients together, spoon over the avocado and grapefruit and garnish each with a twist of lime.

Note: if pink grapefruit is not available, you can substitute a mixture of ordinary grapefruit and orange segments.

Mixed beans with lemon garlic dressing

410g / 14½ oz can flageolets
400g / 14oz can white kidney beans
Dressing
30ml / 2 tablespoons natural quark
15ml / 1 tablespoon olive oil
grated rind and juice of ½ lemon
1 clove garlic, finely chopped
salt and freshly ground black pepper
Garnish
snipped chives

Drain the beans and place in a bowl. Mix the quark, oil, lemon rind and juice together, add the garlic and season with salt and pepper. Stir the dressing into the beans and spoon into a serving dish. Cover and refrigerate for 1 hour before serving. Garnish with the snipped chives.

Note: you can use any left-over cooked beans in this salad: red kidney beans, black-eyed beans or borlotti beans, for example.

Parma ham with melon and figs

1 Charentais or small Ogen melon
8 slices Parma ham
4 figs

Cut the melon in half and remove all the seeds. Slice the melon into 16 thin slices and carefully cut away and discard the skin. Take each slice of Parma ham, cut it in half, and wrap each piece around a slice of melon. Arrange 4 slices of melon on each plate and decorate each with a fig, cut open with 4 slits to resemble a flower.

*A savoury tomato and clam sorbet
is served in a sparkling ice cup to refresh
your palette between courses.*

Tomato sorbet

2 × 300ml / 10 floz cans tomato and clam juice
5ml / 1 teaspoon Worcestershire sauce
1 egg white
small lemon wedges, to garnish

To make the ice cups: place about 2.5cm/ ½in water in 4 small bowls and freeze. When hard, stand a small glass in the centre of each, place something small and heavy inside to weight it down, then fill the space between the glass and bowl with water. Return to the freezer until hard. To remove, take out the weight and fill the glass with warm water to release it from the ice cup. Stand the bowls in warm water and remove the ice cups; store in the freezer until needed.

Mix the tomato and clam juice with the Worcestershire sauce, pour into a shallow container and freeze until slushy. Turn into a chilled bowl and whisk until the large crystals of ice have broken down. Whisk the egg white until stiff and fold into the tomato sorbet. Return to the freezer and freeze until hard. Allow to soften slightly in the refrigerator for 30 minutes before serving in the prepared ice cups garnished with the lemon wedges.

Main courses

*D*elicate pink trout marinated in
lemon juice is tossed in a salad
with colourful peppers and avocado.

Marinated trout salad

4 trout, filleted and skinned
juice of 3 lemons
1 clove garlic, finely chopped
2 carrots
5cm / 2in piece cucumber
½ yellow pepper, thinly sliced
½ red pepper, thinly sliced
50g / 2oz lambs lettuce
1 avocado, peeled and diced
45ml / 3 tablespoons olive oil
freshly ground black pepper
cucumber rings, to garnish

Place the trout fillets in a shallow dish and pour over the lemon juice. Add the garlic and leave to marinate for at least 4 hours – overnight is preferable. With a potato peeler, pare the carrots into thin ribbons and leave in a bowl of iced water for 1 hour. Cut the cucumber lengthways into thin strips. Drain the fish from the marinade and cut into 2.5cm / 1in pieces and mix with the sliced peppers, carrot and cucumber curls, lambs lettuce and avocado. Arrange on 4 plates and drizzle over the olive oil. Grind some pepper over the salad and garnish with the cucumber rings.

*Rollmop herrings and crisp apple
in a creamy dill dressing are fortified
with fiery Russian vodka.*

Scandinavian herring salad

8 rollmop herrings
1 green apple, cored and diced
½ red skinned onion, thinly sliced
15ml / 1 tablespoon chopped dill
150ml / 5 floz soured cream
45ml / 3 tablespoons vodka
freshly ground black pepper
Garnish
chopped dill
pumpernickel bread

Cut the rollmops into 4cm/1½in pieces, and chop the gherkins around which they were rolled. Put into a bowl with the diced apple, onion and chopped dill. Mix the soured cream and vodka together and pour over the salad. Toss gently and then spoon into a serving dish and garnish with the extra chopped dill. Serve with pumpernickel or dark rye bread.

*Slices of smoked mackerel, trout
and salmon make a delectable threesome
served with a red lumpfish sauce.*

Smoked fish platter

2 peppered smoked mackerel fillets
2 cold or hot smoked trout fillets
6 small slices smoked salmon
Sauce
30ml / 2 tablespoons crème fraiche
30ml / 2 tablespoons single cream
1 hard-boiled egg, chopped
15ml / 1 tablespoon red lumpfish
5ml / 1 teaspoon lemon juice
Garnish
lemon slices
parsley

Skin the mackerel fillets, break into neat pieces and arrange them on a platter. Cut the smoked trout into small pieces and arrange them with the mackerel. Cut the smoked salmon slices in half and roll each piece up. Place on the platter and garnish with the lemon slices and parsley. Mix the ingredients for the sauce together and serve separately in a small bowl.

*This classic Italian seafood
dish never fails to evoke the flavours
of the Mediterranean region.*

Insalata di frutti di mare

286g / 10oz jar prepared seafood salad, drained
225g / 8oz peeled prawns
225g / 8oz cooked mussels
12 prawns to garnish
Dressing
90ml / 6 tablespoons green olive oil
30ml / 2 tablespoons lemon juice
15ml / 1 tablespoon capers
15ml / 1 tablespoon chopped parsley
1 small clove garlic
ground black pepper

Drain the prepared seafood salad and put into a bowl with the prawns and mussels. Mix the dressing ingredients together and pour over the salad. Toss and divide between 4 plates and garnish with the whole prawns.

Note: if you prefer you can substitute fresh crabmeat and lobster for the prepared seafood salad, usually bought in jars.

*S*moked salmon and sole marinated
in lime juice are embellished by a smooth
creamy watercress green sauce

Fish roulades with watercress sauce

4 × 125g / 5oz fillets of lemon sole or plaice,
boned and skinned
salt and white pepper
juice of 4 limes
4 medium slices of smoked salmon
Sauce
45ml / 3 tablespoons mayonnaise
45ml / 3 tablespoons single cream
½ bunch watercress, finely chopped
Garnish
½ avocado, peeled, stoned and sliced
sprigs of watercress

Cut the fish fillets in half and lay them in a shallow dish. Season well. Pour over the lime juice, cover and marinate in the refrigerator for at least 4 hours until the fish is opaque. Reserve the marinade. Cut each slice of salmon in half and place a slice on the skin side of each piece of marinated fish. Roll up tightly.

Whisk the mayonnaise, cream and a little of the marinade together, and stir in the chopped watercress. Pour around the fish roulades on 4 individual serving plates and garnish with sliced avocado and a sprig of watercress.

Succulent prawns with slivers of crisp vegetables are tossed together in a soy and honey oriental-style dressing.

Shanghai salad

225g / 8oz beansprouts, roots trimmed
100g / 4oz carrots, coarsely grated
3 sticks celery, finely sliced
15ml / 1 tablespoon finely slivered root ginger
225g / 8oz peeled prawns
½ head Chinese leaves, finely shredded
½ bunch spring onions, cut into shreds
Dressing
60ml / 4 tablespoons sunflower oil
15ml / 1 tablespoon soy sauce
5ml / 1 teaspoon clear honey
30ml / 2 tablespoons lemon juice
Garnish
spring onion tassels

Put the beansprouts, grated carrots, celery, ginger and prawns into a bowl. Make up the dressing and toss the salad ingredients together. Allow to stand for a few minutes.

Mix the Chinese leaves and spring onions together and arrange on a serving plate. Cover with the prawn mixture and serve garnished with spring onion tassels (see page 37).

*S*kewers of monkfish and scallops
are complemented by pastel
pink prawn and green avocado sauces.

Fish brochettes with two colour sauces

8 scallops
500g / 1lb monkfish, cut in chunks
juice of 3 lemons
juice of 3 limes
1 clove garlic, crushed
15ml / 1 tablespoon chopped tarragon
90ml / 6 tablespoons soured cream
90ml / 6 tablespoons single cream
15ml / 1 tablespoon mayonnaise
½ avocado, peeled
5ml / 1 teaspoon lemon juice
75g / 3oz peeled prawns
salt and pepper
Garnish
50g / 2oz peeled prawns
sprigs of tarragon

Wash the scallops and cut off the corals. Cut the white parts in half and mix with the monk-fish. Pour the fruit juice over the fish. Add the garlic and tarragon, cover and marinate for at least 4 hours.

To make the sauces: mix the creams and place half in a blender or food processor with the mayonnaise, avocado and lemon juice. Work to a purée and repeat with the remaining cream mixture and the prawns. Season to taste. Arrange the fish on 4 skewers, serve with the sauces, prawns and tarragon.

*Traditional Japanese-style raw
fish are dipped in a mixture of soyu and
ginger to create an intriguing meal*

Sashimi

1 mackerel, cleaned
1 large plaice fillet
1 salmon steak
1 carrot, cut into fine strips
2 spring onions, cut into fine strips
15ml / 1 tablespoon grated fresh ginger
Japanese soy sauce (shoyu)

Wrap each fish in greaseproof paper and put into the freezer for about 1 hour to chill. With a very sharp knife cut thin slices of mackerel and plaice, and then cut the salmon into thin strips. Arrange the fish decoratively either on a large platter or 4 individual plates. Garnish with the strips of carrot and onion.

Put the ginger into a small bowl and pour over some soy sauce. The fish is dipped in this mixture and then eaten.

Note: chilling the fish makes it easier to slice it really thinly.

*Smoked trout mousse tantalizingly
disguised in a wrapping of smoked salmon
makes a luxurious summer lunch*

Smoked fish surprise

8 small slices smoked salmon
10ml / 2 teaspoons gelatine
45ml / 3 tablespoons water
2 smoked trout, skinned and boned
210ml / 7 floz soured cream
15ml / 1 tablespoon chopped dill
5ml / 1 teaspoon horseradish sauce
2 egg whites
salt and white pepper
Garnish
black lumpfish roe
dill and curly endive

Use the smoked salmon to line 4 small 210ml/ 7 floz pudding basins. Sprinkle the gelatine over the water and dissolve over a pan of simmering water. Leave to cool. Put the smoked trout into a food processor with the soured cream and work until smooth. Stir in the gelatine, dill and horseradish and season with salt and pepper. Whisk the egg whites until stiff and fold carefully into the mousse mixture. Divide the mousse between the 4 lined basins. Chill for at least 2 hours until set, then carefully turn out onto 4 serving plates. Place a little lumpfish and a tiny sprig of dill on top of each mousse and garnish with curly endive.

*Italian-style tuna and beans make
a robust summer lunch – deliciously simple
and earthy peasant food.*

Tonno con fagiole

283g / 10oz can broad beans
425g / 15oz can cannellini beans
½ red skinned onion, finely sliced
2 × 198g / 7oz cans light meat tuna in oil
30ml / 2 tablespoons chopped parsley
Dressing
60ml / 4 tablespoons olive oil
15ml / 1 tablespoon red wine vinegar
freshly ground black pepper
Garnish
black olives
flat leaved parsley

Rinse the beans and drain in a sieve. Place them in a bowl with the onion. Add the tuna, carefully breaking it up into large flakes with a fork. Mix the dressing and pour over the salad. Add the chopped parsley and toss well. Spoon onto a serving dish and garnish with black olives and flat leaved parsley.

Salade Niçoise

1 lettuce, shredded
538g / 1lb 3oz can new potatoes, drained and diced
4 spring onions, chopped
75ml / 5 tablespoons mayonnaise
200g / 7oz can tuna in oil, drained
283g / 10oz can cut green beans
4 tomatoes, chopped
2 hard-boiled eggs, chopped
50g / 1¾oz can anchovies, drained
8 black olives
15ml / 1 tablespoon chopped parsley
Dressing
45ml / 3 tablespoons olive oil
15ml / 1 tablespoon white wine vinegar
salt and freshly ground pepper

Place the shredded lettuce on an oval platter. Put the diced potatoes, spring onions and mayonnaise in a bowl and mix together; then spoon over the lettuce, mounding slightly in the middle. Break up the tuna and arrange in the centre. Add a row of beans on each side, then a row of chopped tomatoes beside the beans. Spoon the chopped egg at each end of the salad. Arrange the anchovies in a lattice pattern over the tuna fish, then garnish with the black olives. Make the dressing and spoon over the salad. Sprinkle with chopped parsley and serve.

Spanish salad

350g / 12oz cooked rice, or frozen rice, thawed
225g / 8oz cooked chicken, diced
100g / 4oz chorizo sausage, sliced
225g / 8oz mussels in brine, drained
4 spring onions, chopped
1 red pepper, seeded and thinly sliced
100g / 4oz frozen peas, thawed
Dressing
45ml / 3 tablespoons olive oil
15ml / 1 tablespoon red wine vinegar
10ml / 2 teaspoons paprika
1 clove garlic, crushed
salt and freshly ground black pepper
Garnish
75g / 3oz whole prawns
lemon wedges

Put the rice, chicken, sausage, mussels, spring onions, red pepper and peas in a bowl and mix together. Make the dressing and pour over the salad. Toss gently and then transfer to a serving dish. Garnish with the whole prawns and lemon wedges.

*This is duck à l'orange with
a difference – smoked duck served with
a colourful continental salad.*

Smoked duck and orange salad

4 smoked duck breasts or 1 whole smoked duck
1 box mixed continental salad (e.g. radicchio,
batavia, lamb's lettuce, curly endive and chicory)
2 small oranges, peeled and segmented
25g / 1oz toasted chopped hazelnuts
Dressing
30ml / 2 tablespoons hazelnut oil
15ml / 1 tablespoon sunflower oil
15ml / 1 tablespoon white wine vinegar
salt and ground black pepper
Accompaniment
bigarade sauce

Slice the duck and arrange neatly on 4 plates. Mix the salad leaves with the orange segments and divide between the plates. Mix the dressing ingredients together and drizzle over the salad. Sprinkle with chopped hazelnuts and serve accompanied with the bigarade sauce.

Note: you can buy bigarade sauce in good delicatessens. Otherwise use Cumberland sauce or a good orange relish. Most supermarket chains now sell boxes of continental salad. Otherwise, you can mix fresh salad leaves of your choice.

*S*liced Parma ham, mozzarella and avocado
all reflect the red, white
and green of the Italian national flag.

Tricolore salad

4 large tomatoes, sliced
½ Spanish onion, sliced
225g / 8oz mozzarella cheese, sliced
1 avocado, stoned, peeled and sliced
8 thin slices Parma ham
Dressing
45ml / 3 tablespoons olive oil
15ml / 1 tablespoon wine vinegar
pinch of sugar
10ml / 2 teaspoons chopped fresh basil
salt and ground black pepper
Garnish
black olives
sprigs of basil

On 4 dinner plates, arrange first a layer of tomato, then a layer of onion, next some slices of cheese and avocado and then top with rolls of Parma ham. Mix the dressing and dribble over each salad. Garnish with black olives and the sprigs of basil.

*T*ender oak-smoked chicken and
juicy peaches are arranged in a star shape
with a raspberry vinegar dressing.

Smoked chicken salad

½ curly endive
½ webbs lettuce
4 smoked chicken breasts
3 peaches or nectarines
4 raspberries to garnish
Dressing
15ml / 1 tablespoon raspberry vinegar
15ml / 1 tablespoon olive oil
30ml / 2 tablespoons sunflower oil
salt and freshly ground black pepper

Wash, dry and tear the endive and webbs lettuce into manageable pieces and divide between 4 plates. Slice the chicken and peaches and arrange on top of the lettuce as shown in the picture opposite. Mix together the vinegar and oils, season with salt and pepper and sprinkle over the salads. Garnish each with a raspberry and serve immediately.

Steak tartar

500g / 1lb fillet steak
30ml / 2 tablespoons sunflower oil
2 cloves garlic, finely chopped
2.5ml / ½ teaspoon Tabasco sauce
salt and freshly ground black pepper
4 egg yolks, in their half shells
1 small onion, chopped
30ml / 2 tablespoons chopped parsley
30ml / 2 tablespoons capers, chopped
1 red pepper, seeded and finely chopped
Garnish
lettuce
mayonnaise

Finely chop or mince the steak, then add the oil, garlic and Tabasco. Season with salt and pepper, mix well and form into 4 rounds. Place on 4 individual plates, make a shallow indentation in the middle of each round and put the egg yolk in its half shell inside. Arrange small piles of the onion, parsley, capers and red pepper around each round of steak tartar, and then garnish with lettuce. Serve with mayonnaise.

Indian chicken salad

3 breasts cooked tandoori chicken
432g / 15¼ oz chick peas, drained
½ iceberg lettuce, shredded
½ cucumber, sliced
4 tomatoes, sliced
50g / 2oz toasted cashew nuts
Dressing
150ml / 5 floz natural yoghurt
15ml / 1 tablespoon chopped mint
salt and freshly ground black pepper

Cut the chicken into small thickish slices and place in a bowl with the chick peas. Make the dressing: mix the yoghurt and mint together and season with salt and pepper. Pour over the chicken and toss together. Arrange the shredded lettuce on a serving plate and pile the chicken salad on top. Place alternate slices of cucumber and tomato around the edge. Scatter with toasted cashew nuts and serve.

*Italian pastrami, tender artichoke
hearts and crisp radish 'concertinas' combine
to make a dazzling burst of colour.*

Beef and radish salad

1 bunch radishes
225g / 8oz pastrami, cut into strips
1 shallot, finely chopped
1 lettuce, shredded
400g / 14oz artichoke hearts, drained and halved
Dressing
45ml / 3 tablespoons olive oil
15ml / 1 tablespoon red wine vinegar
1 small clove garlic, crushed
15ml / 1 tablespoon poppy seeds
salt and freshly ground pepper

Trim the radishes and then make several cuts in each one to give a concertina effect. Put the radishes in a bowl of iced water to help them open up.

In another bowl, mix together the pastrami, shallot, lettuce and artichoke hearts. Mix the dressing ingredients together and pour over the salad. Toss well, transfer to a serving dish and garnish with the radishes. *Note:* You can use left-over cold roast beef or salt beef instead of pastrami.

*E*xotic kiwi fruit, mange-tout and
colourful red and yellow peppers are the perfect
accompaniment for spicy turkey.

Devilled turkey and mange-tout salad

175g / 6oz mange-tout
350g / 12oz cooked turkey, cut into
bite-sized pieces
1 red pepper, seeded and diced
1 yellow pepper, seeded and diced
25g / 1oz pinenuts
Dressing
60ml / 4 tablespoons sunflower oil
15ml / 1 tablespoon wine vinegar
5ml / 1 teaspoon Worcestershire sauce
2.5ml / ½ teaspoon paprika
2.5ml / ½ teaspoon mustard
pinch of ground cumin
salt and ground black pepper
Garnish
1 kiwi fruit, peeled and sliced

Cut the mange-tout in half and place in a bowl. Pour over boiling water and leave to stand for 2 minutes, then rinse under cold water and drain. Place in a salad bowl with the other ingredients. Make up the dressing and pour over the salad and toss together. Divide between 4 dishes and garnish with the slices of kiwi fruit.

*Colourful layers of seasonal
vegetables are artistically revealed in a
ring of clear aspic set for viewing.*

Summer vegetable ring

150ml / 5 floz dry white wine
25g / 1oz sachet aspic jelly crystals
450ml / 15 floz cold water
340g / 12oz can asparagus spears
3 young carrots
2 young courgettes, thinly sliced
2 tomatoes, skinned, quartered and seeded
8 black olives
75g / 3oz petit pois, thawed if frozen

In a saucepan, heat the wine until hot, sprinkle over the aspic crystals and stir until dissolved. Then add the cold water. Pour a little of the aspic into the bottom of a 900ml/ 1½ pint ring mould. Cut the tips off the asparagus spears and arrange them in the bottom of the mould, then refrigerate until set. Meanwhile, pour boiling water over the carrots and leave to stand for 3 minutes. Do likewise with the courgettes and leave for 1 minute. Drain the vegetables and allow to cool. Arrange the vegetables in the mould with the tomatoes, olives and peas. Chop up the rest of the asparagus and place on top. Carefully pour the aspic into the mould. Return to the refrigerator and leave to set.

To serve: dip the mould in a bowl of hot water for 10 seconds, then invert onto a serving plate, giving the mould a little shake to release the jelly.

*A trio of three different salamis,
peppers and olives makes a typically
Italian cold platter for lunch.*

Italian pepper and salami salad

1 green pepper
1 red pepper
1 yellow pepper
100g / 4oz pepper salami
75g / 3oz salami tipo Milano
75g / 3oz coppa tipo Parma
black olives
Dressing
45ml / 3 tablespoons olive oil
15ml / 1 tablespoon wine vinegar
1 clove garlic, finely chopped
salt and freshly ground black pepper

Place the peppers under a really hot grill, turning them until the skins are brown and blistered. Leave until cool enough to handle and then peel away the skin. Cut the peppers in half lengthways and remove the seeds. Cut into thin strips and place in a container. Mix the ingredients for the dressing and pour over the peppers. Cover and leave to marinate for at least 2 hours.

To serve: arrange the salamis on a platter with the strips of pepper and garnish with black olives. Spoon a little of the dressing over the peppers before serving.

*Tiny balls of sweet cream cheese
studded with walnuts contrast deliciously
with bitter spinach leaves.*

Cheese and walnut salad

225g / 8oz cream cheese
100g / 4oz walnuts, chopped
225g / 8oz young spinach, washed
3 sticks celery, sliced
5cm / 2in piece cucumber, diced
1 green dessert apple, cored and diced
30ml / 2 tablespoons lemon juice
30ml / 2 tablespoons walnut oil
salt and freshly ground pepper

Make the cream cheese balls by taking tea-spoons of cheese and rolling them into balls. Lightly roll these balls in the chopped walnuts and leave in the refrigerator until needed.

Drain as much water from the spinach as possible and put in a salad bowl with the celery and cucumber. Toss the apple in the lemon juice, drain and add to the salad. Mix the walnut oil with the remaining lemon juice, season well and pour over the salad. Toss the ingredients together. To serve: place the cheese balls in the salad.

*Curried quail's eggs form the centre
of a colourful flower with chicken,
mango and red pepper petals.*

Celebration salad

4 cooked chicken breasts
2 mangoes, peeled and sliced
1 red pepper, seeded and sliced
½ small carton alfalfa sprouts
12 quail's eggs, hard-boiled
paprika to garnish
Dressing
60ml / 4 tablespoons mayonnaise
30ml / 2 tablespoons natural yoghurt
5ml / 1 teaspoon curry paste
15ml / 1 tablespoon mango chutney

Slice the chicken breasts and arrange them on
4 plates. Arrange the mango and red pepper
slices around each plate with the chicken.
Place a nest of alfalfa sprouts in the centre
with three shelled quail's eggs on each. Make
up the dressing by mixing all the ingredients
together until well-blended and then spoon-
ing it over the eggs. Serve sprinkled with a
little paprika on each.

*A crunchy mixture of chick peas,
tomato and mushroom makes a healthy filling
for vividly coloured peppers.*

Summer stuffed peppers

4 medium-sized red peppers
4 medium-sized yellow peppers
432g / 15¼oz can chick peas, drained
75g / 3oz button mushrooms, chopped
3 tomatoes, chopped
5 spring onions, chopped
30ml / 2 tablespoons sunflower seeds
Dressing
45ml / 3 tablespoons sunflower oil
15ml / 1 tablespoon cider vinegar
2.5ml / ½ teaspoon mustard
15ml / 1 tablespoon chopped mixed fresh herbs
salt and ground black pepper

Cut the peppers in half lengthways and remove the seeds. In a bowl, mix the chick
peas, mushrooms, tomatoes, spring onions
and sunflower seeds together. Whisk the
ingredients for the dressing, pour over the
chick pea mixture and toss together. Divide
between the pepper halves and serve with a
crisp green salad.

Desserts

Skewered strawberries, papaya and kumquats are unusuual fruit brochettes enlivened by a strawberry roulé sauce.

Exotic fruit brochettes with strawberry dip

225g / 8oz strawberries
1 papaya, peeled and cubed
4 kumquats
Sauce
213g / 7½oz can strawberries, drained
or 100g / 4oz ripe strawberries
225g / 8oz strawberry roulé cheese

Prepare the fruit and arrange alternately on thin bamboo skewers, reserving 4 strawberries for decoration. For the sauce: put the strawberries and roulé cheese into a blender or processor and blend until smooth. Place a brochette and a good spoonful of sauce on each of 4 plates and decorate with the reserved strawberries.
Note: you can use any exotic fruits on these brochettes. For instance, mangoes, guavas, stoned lychees and kiwi fruit are all suitable.

*F*lamboyantly coloured summer fruits
flavoured with kirsch liqueur
are piled high in a fresh pineapple boat.

Pineapple fruit salad

2 small pineapples
175g / 6oz strawberries, halved
100g / 4oz raspberries, thawed if frozen
100g / 4oz seedless green grapes
1 kiwi fruit, peeled and diced
60ml / 4 tablespoons kirsch

Halve the pineapples and cut around the sides to remove the inner flesh with a serrated knife, leaving a shell about 1.5cm / ½in thick. Using a spoon, scoop out the inside of each half, cut away and discard the hard central core and dice the flesh. Place the pineapple in a bowl with the other fruit and pour the kirsch over the top. Mix well and chill in the refrigerator for 1 hour.

To serve: divide the fruit between the pine-apple shells and place each on a serving plate.

*Semi-dried figs and sliced orange
topped with kumquats are captured in an
abstract mood for a winter dessert.*

Figs à l'orange

Serves 6 - 8

350g / 12oz semi-dried figs
5 oranges
45ml / 3 tablespoons orange liqueur (optional)
3 kumquats, sliced

Rinse the figs in a sieve under a running tap to remove the flour coating. Put in a bowl and cover with boiling water. Leave to stand for at least 3 hours, or overnight.

In the meantime, using a zester, cut thin strips of rind from one of the oranges, place in a small bowl and cover with boiling water. Leave to stand for 30 minutes, drain and set aside. Squeeze the juice from this orange and mix with 120ml / 4floz of the soaking liquid from the figs, discarding the rest. Peel and slice the remaining oranges and place in a serving bowl with the figs. Pour over the juice and liqueur (if using) and mix together. Scatter over the strips of orange rind and the slices of kumquat before serving.

Note: if semi-dried figs are not available, use canned ones.

*F*resh fruits nestle atop an ice
mountain towering above a dark pool of rich
chocolate sauce for dipping.

Fruity ice mountain with chocolate dip

Lots of ice cubes
500g / 1lb fresh fruit, e.g. strawberries, kiwi fruit,
grapes, satsumas, cherries, pineapple and peaches
Dip
100g / 4oz plain chocolate
150ml / 5 floz double cream
30ml / 2 tablespoons apricot brandy

Fill a 1.5 litre / 2½ pint ring mould with water and freeze until solid. Dip the mould quickly in and out of warm water to release the ring of ice. Crush lots of ice cubes and press the crushed ice onto the ice ring, filling the centre and levelling the top. Refreeze and then add more crushed ice to give a rough surface.

To make the dip: place the chocolate in a bowl and stand it over a pan of hot water until it melts. Stir in the cream and apricot brandy. Prepare the fruit of your choice, removing any pips or stones and chop the flesh into bite-sized pieces. Arrange the fruit all over the ice mountain (it should stick) and serve the chocolate dip separately.

Note: the ice mountain can be made well in advance and kept in the freezer until needed. It can be re-used several times by pressing on more crushed ice and refreezing.

*A spectacular Catherine wheel
of sliced fresh peaches spins in a delicious
raspberry sauce with cream swirls.*

Peaches royal

350g / 12oz raspberries, thawed if frozen
50g / 2oz icing sugar
4 large peaches
mint leaves
20ml / 4 teaspoons single cream

Reserve 4 raspberries and press the rest through a sieve to give a smooth purée. Stir in the icing sugar to sweeten. Slice the peaches, discarding the stones, and arrange each one attractively on a plate. Carefully pour the raspberry sauce around the peaches and decorate with the reserved raspberries and mint leaves. Using a teaspoon, drop small blobs of cream onto the raspberry sauce. Take a skewer and pull through the cream to make attractive wisps.

*Scoops of lemon sorbet and melon
are served with a surprise taste of Galliano
liqueur for balmy summer days.*

Melon and lemon sundaes

500ml / 18floz lemon sorbet
1 large honeydew melon
strips of rind of 1 lemon
90ml / 6 tablespoons Galliano liqueur

Using a melon baller, scoop out the sorbet onto a tray lined with non-stick paper. Work quickly, then return the balls to the freezer to harden up. Scoop out the melon with the baller, collecting the juice in a bowl. Put the melon balls in the juice, then sprinkle over the lemon rind and set aside until you are ready to make up the dessert. Put the sundae glasses in the refrigerator and chill the liqueur. Drain the melon balls, then quickly layer up with the lemon sorbet balls in the sundae glasses. Decorate with the strips of lemon rind. Pour over the Galliano and serve immediately.

*Exotic lychees and sharon fruit
make a mouthwatering mousse topped with
a flutter of sugared rose petals.*

Oriental mousse

Serves 6

10ml / 2 teaspoons gelatine
2 sharon fruit
15ml / 1 tablespoon lemon juice
30ml / 2 tablespoons caster sugar
300ml / 10 floz whipping cream
12 lychees, peeled and stoned
1 egg white
4 kiwi fruit, peeled and sliced
Decoration
rose petals, egg white, caster sugar

In a small bowl, sprinkle the gelatine over 45ml / 3 tablespoons water and leave to become spongy. Set over a pan of hot water and leave until dissolved. Remove the skin from the sharon fruit and put the flesh into a blender or food processor with the lemon juice and sugar. Work to a purée, add the gelatine and mix together.

Whip the cream until softly peaking, fold in the fruit purée and the lychees. Whisk the egg white until stiff and fold into the cream mixture. Pour into a glass serving dish and arrange the slices of kiwi fruit around the edge. Place in the refrigerator to chill.

To make the sugared rose petals, separate the petals and brush with egg white. Coat with caster sugar, place on greaseproof paper and leave to dry. Use to decorate the mousse.

Ginger-flavoured mango ice is spooned into flower-shaped bitter chocolate cups for maximum effect.

Chocolate mango cups

425g / 15oz can mango slices in syrup
50g / 2oz caster sugar
5ml / 1 teaspoon ginger purée or 1 piece of stem
ginger, finely chopped
150ml / 5fl oz natural yoghurt
4 chocolate cups

Put the mango and its juice into a blender or food processor with the sugar and ginger. Blend to make a purée. Fold in the yoghurt, pour into a container and freeze until slushy. Tip the mango ice into a bowl and whisk to break down the ice crystals. Return to the container and freeze until firm. To serve: refrigerate for 30 minutes and then scoop the mango ice into 4 chocolate cups. Serve accompanied with chocolate wafer biscuits.
Note: You can buy ready-made chocolate cups, but if you wish to make your own, just melt some good-quality plain chocolate and pour into fluted paper cases (three thick). Use the back of a spoon to coat the sides. Leave to set and then apply another thin coat of chocolate. When the cups are hard, remove the paper.

*F*resh raspberries and cream are
whipped up in just minutes to create a
spectacular marbled dessert.

Chilled raspberry parfait

500g / 1lb raspberries, thawed if frozen
2 egg whites
100g / 4oz caster sugar
300ml / 10floz double cream
12 raspberries to decorate
palmier sweet biscuits

Press the raspberries through a sieve to remove the pips. Leave the purée in the freezer for 2-3 hours until firmly mushy. Just before serving, whisk the egg whites until stiff and gradually whisk in the sugar. Whip the cream until it stands in soft peaks and fold into the egg whites. Remove the raspberry purée from the freezer and turn into a bowl. Break it up with a wooden spoon, and then whisk to create a semi-frozen mixture. Fold into the cream and spoon into 4 glasses. Decorate with raspberries and serve with small sweet biscuits such as palmiers.

*A̲lthough this looks sensational, this
is simplicity itself to make – just coffee flavoured
whipped cream, meringues and fruit.*

Coffee meringue delight

Serves 6 - 8

15ml / 1 tablespoon instant coffee
45ml / 3 tablespoons Tia Maria
60ml / 4 tablespoons icing sugar
300ml / 10 floz double cream
175g / 6oz seedless grapes
100g / 4oz small meringues

Dissolve the instant coffee in 15ml / 1 table-spoon boiling water and mix with the Tia Maria. Put the icing sugar and cream in a bowl and whisk until softly peaking. Add the coffee mixture and whisk again. Place the cream in a piping bag fitted with a star nozzle. Arrange some of the meringues in a 20cm / 8in circle on a plate and pipe a rosette of cream between each. Place some more mer-ingues in the middle and pipe some cream between them, placing some grapes in the cream. Layer up the meringues and cream with the grapes in progressively smaller circles to from a pyramid, decorating the top with grapes.

*Strawberry flavoured fromage frais
makes a beautiful cheesecake and is topped
with fresh strawberries galore.*

Strawberry cheesecake

50g / 2oz unsalted butter
175g / 6oz almond or Viennese biscuits, crushed
12.5g / ½oz gelatine
30ml / 2 tablespoons water
2 x 200g / 7oz jars or cartons strawberry
fromage frais
150ml / ¼ pint double cream
2 egg whites
To decorate
225g / 8oz fresh strawberries, halved
150ml / ¼ pint double cream, whipped

Melt the butter and stir in the crushed biscuits. Press into the base of a 20cm / 8in loose-bottomed spring form cake tin. Sprinkle the gelatine over the water and dissolve over a pan of hot water. Allow to cool a little before whisking into the cheese (fromage frais). Whip the cream until floppy and fold it into the cheese mixture. Whisk the egg whites until stiff and carefully fold into the mixture. Turn the filling into the tin and refrigerate until set. To serve, release the cheesecake and transfer to a serving plate. Arrange the strawberries on top and decorate the edge with piped whipped cream.

The name means 'little pumpkin'
but this is anything but — a rich concoction of
chocolate, cherries and whipped cream.

Zucotta

500g / 1lb chocolate cake
60ml / 4 tablespoons brandy
60ml / 4 tablespoons sweet liqueur, e.g. cherry
brandy or Amaretto
600ml / 1 pint whipping cream
100g / 4oz icing sugar, sieved
50g / 2oz blanched almonds, toasted and chopped
100g / 4oz dessert chocolate, grated
225g / 8oz black cherries, stoned and halved
Decoration
cocoa powder
icing sugar
a few extra cherries

Cut the cake into slices or fingers and use three-quarters to line a 1.8 litre / 3 pint flattish pudding basin. Mix together the brandy and liqueur and sprinkle over the sponge.

Whip three-quarters of the cream with the icing sugar until stiff, and then fold in the chopped nuts, the chocolate and the cherries. Fill the lined basin with the cream mixture and cover with the remaining cake. Cover the bowl and chill for several hours.

To serve, run a knife around the edge of the pudding to loosen it and then invert a flat-bottomed plate over the mould. Turn out and decorate the top with cocoa powder and icing sugar in alternate segments. Whip the remaining cream and pipe it around the base of the cake. Serve immediately, decorated with extra cherries.

*A flash of Italian inspiration –
celebrated Panettone cake is filled with layers
of chocolate and tutti frutti ice-cream.*

Italian ice-cream·cake

500g / 1lb Italian Panettone cake
90ml / 3floz medium sweet sherry
1 small carton rich chocolate ice-cream
1 small carton tutti frutti ice-cream

Using a sharp knife, cut a 1cm/½in thick slice off the bottom of the cake and set aside. Carefully scoop out the centre of the cake leaving a shell 1cm/½in thick. Put the inside of the cake into a blender or food processor and process down into crumbs. Tip them into a bowl and stir in the sherry. Slightly soften the chocolate ice-cream and spoon enough into the hollow of the cake to fill it just less than one-third, pressing the ice-cream well down and into the sides. Spoon over half of the soaked cake crumbs and press down.

Add enough tutti frutti ice-cream to come two-thirds up the sides of the cake and cover with the remaining crumbs, pressing down. Add another layer of chocolate ice-cream and cover with the reserved slice of cake. Wrap the cake in foil and return to the freezer to store until needed.

To serve the cake: remove from the freezer about 30 minutes before serving and place in the refrigerator to allow it to soften slightly. Serve cut into thin slices.

Note: Panettone cake can be purchased in Italian delicatessens.

*Wickedly rich but irresistible,
this uncooked chocolate and marzipan cake is
flavoured with rum and cherries.*

Chocolate marzipan cake

Serves 8-10

225g / 8oz plain chocolate
100g / 4oz unsalted butter
2 eggs
30ml / 2 tablespoons rum or brandy
225g / 8oz shortcake biscuits, broken into
small pieces
175g / 6oz golden marzipan, diced
75g / 3oz glacé cherries, chopped
To decorate
icing sugar
grated chocolate
25g / 1oz glacé cherries, chopped into small pieces

Put the chocolate and butter in a bowl and stand over a pan of hot water until melted. Whisk the eggs until frothy and then whisk into the melted chocolate mixture with the rum. Stir in the broken biscuits, the marzipan and cherries and mix well. Turn into a 23cm / 9in loose-bottomed flan tin and press the mixture down well. Level the top and refrigerate for at least 2 hours to set. Remove from the tin and slide onto a serving plate. Lightly dust with icing sugar and decorate with the grated chocolate and chopped cherries.

*Sparkling jewels of glacé and
sugared fruits shine out of a mountain of
fabulous creamy rice pudding.*

Jewelled rice dessert

Serves 8

425g / 15oz can rice pudding
100g / 4oz fresh dates, skinned, stoned
and chopped
50g / 2oz glacé cherries, chopped
150g / 5oz sugared fruit, chopped
20g / ¾oz gelatine
2.5ml / ½ teaspoon vanilla essence
1 egg white
150ml / 5floz whipping cream
To decorate
90ml / 3floz whipping cream
2 glacé cherries, cut into small pieces

Mix the rice pudding with the chopped dates and fruit. In a small bowl, sprinkle the gelatine over 75ml / 5 tablespoons water and leave to soak. When spongy, dissolve over a pan of hot water. Stir into the rice mixture with the vanilla essence. Whisk the egg white until stiff and whip the cream until floppy. Fold them into the mixture and pour into a wetted 900ml / 1½ pint jelly mould. Chill in the refrigerator until set and then turn out onto a serving plate. Whip the rest of the cream and pipe a decoration around the dessert finishing with tiny pieces of cherry.
Note: sugared fruit is similar to glacé fruit. It is usually imported from Spain.

*Creamy individual soufflés of
apple purée and crème de menthe liqueur
make a deliciously refreshing dessert.*

Apple mint soufflés

15g / ½oz gelatine
3 large eggs, separated
50g / 2oz caster sugar
350g / 12oz jar cooked apple, mashed roughly
45ml / 3 tablespoons crème de menthe
150ml / 5floz whipping cream
toasted chopped nuts
sprigs of mint

Prepare 4 ramekin dishes by tying a double band of greaseproof paper around each to come 5cm/2in above the rim. Put 45ml/3 tablespoons of water in a small bowl and sprinkle over the gelatine. Leave it to become spongy and then dissolve over a pan of hot water. Set aside to cool slightly.

Put the egg yolks and sugar in a bowl and whisk until thick and creamy. Fold into the apple with the crème de menthe and stir in the gelatine. Whip the cream until floppy and fold into the apple mixture. Whisk the egg whites until stiff, fold in and pour the soufflé mixture into the prepared dishes. Refrigerate until set. Remove the paper bands and press the chopped nuts onto the sides. Place a sprig of mint on top of each and serve.

*Blackcurrants, pears and guavas make
a pretty trio of sorbets – deceptively
simple to prepare yet delicious to eat.*

A trio of sorbets

Blackcurrant
500g / 1lb blackcurrants, fresh or thawed if frozen
100g / 4oz icing sugar
45ml / 3 tablespoons cassis
1 egg white, stiffly whisked

Sieve the blackcurrants and stir in the icing sugar, cassis and 150ml / 5floz water. Freeze until slushy. Whisk to break down the crystals and fold in the egg white. Freeze.

Pear and wine
411g / 14½oz can pears in syrup
150ml / 5floz medium sweet white wine

Put the pears and wine in a blender or food processor and work until smooth. Freeze until slushy. Whisk, cover and freeze.

Guava
411g / 14½oz can guavas in syrup
juice of 1 orange
1 egg white, stiffly whisked

Blend the guavas and syrup in a blender or food processor with the orange juice. Sieve and freeze until slushy. Whisk until smooth. Fold in the egg white and freeze.

*A marbled swirl of yoghurt adds
the finishing touch to this apricot concoction
in a crisp brandysnap case.*

Amaretto apricot flan

Serves 6

100g / 4oz petit beurre biscuits
100g / 4oz brandy snaps
75g / 3oz butter, melted
Filling
175g / 6oz semi-dried apricots
45ml / 3 tablespoons Amaretto liqueur
10ml / 2 teaspoons gelatine
60ml / 4 tablespoons natural yoghurt
15ml / 1 tablespoon toasted flaked almonds

To make the flan case: crush the biscuits and brandy snaps and mix into the melted butter. Press into a 20cm / 8in loose-bottomed flan case and refrigerate to set. In the meantime, cover the apricots with boiling water and leave to soak for 2 hours.

Place the soaked apricots in a blender or food processor with 120ml / 4floz of the soaking liquid and the liqueur and work to a purèe. Measure 30ml / 2 tablespoons of the soaking liquid into a small bowl and sprinkle over the gelatine. When it has become spongy, dissolve over a pan of hot water. Stir the gelatine into the apricot mixture, pour into the biscuit case and swirl in the yoghurt. Return to the refrigerator to chill. Remove the flan carefully from the tin, scatter with flaked almonds and serve.

*O*range and Drambuie flavoured
chocolate mousse sits in a neat border of
orange-dipped sponge fingers.

Chocolate charlotte

Serves 8

16 sponge fingers
juice of 1 orange
225g / 8oz plain chocolate
15g / ½oz gelatine
45ml / 3 tablespoons Drambuie
50g / 2oz sugar
2 egg yolks
300ml / 10floz whipping cream, whipped
1 egg white, whisked stiffly
Decoration
150ml / 5floz double cream, whipped

Grease and line the base of a 1.75 litre / 3 pint charlotte tin. Dip the sponge fingers into the orange juice. Arrange around the sides of the tin, sugar side out. Melt the chocolate over a pan of hot water. Place some non-stick baking paper on a tray and spread with 45ml / 3 table-spoons of chocolate. Set aside to harden.

Meanwhile, sprinkle the gelatine into 75ml / 5 tablespoons water and leave until spongy. Dissolve over a pan of hot water. Beat the remaining orange juice and Drambuie into the chocolate. Whisk the egg yolks and sugar until thick and beat into the chocolate with the gelatine. Fold in the cream and egg white and pour into the tin and refrigerate until set. Using a fancy cutter, cut out some chocolate shapes. To serve: turn out of the tin, pipe the cream around the edge and decorate with chocolate shapes.

A single cheesecake heart topped with frosted fruit sits seductively in a pool of clear redcurrant sauce

Cheesecake hearts

175g / 6oz curd cheese
50g / 2oz caster sugar
5ml / 1 teaspoon grated lemon rind
10ml / 2 teaspoons lemon juice
1 egg, separated
10ml / 2 teaspoons gelatine
Sauce
225g / 8oz redcurrants, thawed if frozen
50g / 2oz icing sugar
15ml / 1 tablespoon caster sugar
sprigs mint

Lightly oil the bases of 4 heart shaped dishes. If there are holes in them, cover with grease-proof paper. Put the curd cheese, sugar, lemon rind and juice and egg yolk into a bowl and beat together until smooth. Dissolve the gelatine in 30ml / 2 tablespoons water over a pan of hot water and stir into the cheese mixture. Whisk the egg white until stiff and fold into the mixture. Divide between the dishes and chill until set. Reserve 12 redcurrants, and press the rest through a sieve to make a purée. Stir in the icing sugar.

To serve, loosen the edges of the cheese-cakes with a knife and turn out on to individual serving plates. Pour the redcurrant sauce around each cheesecake. Dip the reserved red-currants in the caster sugar and use to decorate the hearts finishing each with a sprig of mint.

Index

Numerals in *italics* refer to illustrations.

Acknowledgements

We would like to thank David Burch for taking the photographs in this book and Lorna Rhodes for preparing the food for photography.
We also wish to extend our gratitude to the following suppliers for their kindness in lending items for photography:
Amtico Tiles : ceramic tiles
The Boots Company : table linen
Chinacraft : china
Kilkenny Design : linen and crockery
David Mellor : cutlery
Next : table linen
Wedgwood : china